AF586770

WORKING PAPER
ALFRED P. SLOAN SCHOOL OF MANAGEMENT

Managing Data Quality:
A Critical Issue for the Decade to Come

Mark D. Hansen
Y. Richard Wang

March 1991, Sloan WP # 3253-91-MSA
CIS WP # CIS-91-01

MASSACHUSETTS
INSTITUTE OF TECHNOLOGY
50 MEMORIAL DRIVE
CAMBRIDGE, MASSACHUSETTS 02139

Managing Data Quality:
A Critical Issue for the Decade to Come

Mark D Hansen
Y Richard Wang

March 1991, Sloan WP # 3253-91-MSA
CIS WP # CIS-91-01

Composite Information Systems Laboratory
E53-320, Sloan School of Management
Massachusetts Institute of Technology
Cambridge, Mass 02139
ATTN. Prof Richard Wang
(617) 253-0442
Bitnet Address: rwang@sloan mit edu

ACKNOWLEDGEMENTS The authors would like to thank Robert P Goldberg for his encouragement and inspiration throughout this research Thanks are also due to Eileen Glovsky and Sarah King for conducting field work and contributing ideas during the early stages of this project and Dae-Chul Sohn for his assistance Research conducted by Richard Wang has been supported, in part, by MIT's International Financial Services Research Center and MIT's Center for Information Systems Research

Managing Data Quality:
A Critical Issue for the Decade to Come

ABSTRACT This paper presents a study of data quality in the context of the information systems organization We introduce a fundamental analogy between manufacturing and information systems, define the dimensions of data quality, and develop the concept of a *data value chain*. Based on these ideas, we analyze the impact of data quality on corporate profits and present the results of a detailed field study. The study reveals an urgent need to improve Corporate America's data quality along four dimensions accuracy, interpretability, availability, and timeliness A majority of field study participants also expressed difficulty tracking down the sources of their data quality problems Finally, we argue that organizations can realize significant economic benefits from the proper management of data quality. Toward that end, we develop a five-phase methodology for managing data quality and identify five critical success factors for operationalizing data quality management

This study has raised many intriguing research issues. Example. What kinds of technologies can be developed to certify existing corporate data, to certify external sources of data, and to provide data auditability? How should data originators, data distributors, and data consumers manage data quality problems differently? How can procedures and technologies for data quality be managed in the context of overall architectures for data administration? What critical issues need to be addressed in developing and installing data warehouses? With the evident trends in systems integration, data architectures, and the proliferation of management support systems, Corporate America will be confronted with these critical research issues in the decade to come.

Managing Data Quality:
A Critical Issue for the Decade to Come

1. Introduction

Significant advances in the price, speed-performance, capacity, and capabilities of new database and telecommunication technologies have created a wide range of opportunities for corporations to align their information technology for competitive advantage in the marketplace. Across industries such as banking, insurance, retail, consumer marketing, and health care, the capabilities to access databases containing market, manufacturing, and financial information are becoming increasingly critical (Cash & Konsynski, 1985; Clemens, 1988; Goodhue, Quillard, & Rockart, 1988; Henderson, 1989; Ives & Learmonth, 1984; Keen, 1986; Madnick, Osborn, & Wang, 1990; Madnick & Wang, 1988; McFarlan, 1984).

1.1 Data Quality: A Vital Economic Issue

It has been concluded that corporations in the 1990s will integrate their business processes across traditional functional, product, and geographic lines (Scott Morton, 1989). The integration of business processes, in turn, will accelerate demands for more effective Management Support Systems for product development, product delivery, and customer service and management (Rockart & Short, 1989). Significantly, many important Management Support Systems require access to and seamless integration of corporate functional, product, and geographic databases. As a result, poor data quality within single databases, and more significantly across multiple databases where data flow through the *data value chain*, can have a substantial impact on corporate profits. For example, inaccurate data accessed by American Airline's reservation system cost the firm $50 million dollars in lost bookings during the summer of 1988.[1]

U.S. corporations have learned that they need to improve the quality of their products (Crosby, 1979; Garvin, 1983; Garvin, 1988). Many corporations have devoted significant time and energy to upgrade their quality by adopting programs to implement a variety of initiatives involving cost of quality measurements, interfunctional teams, reliability engineering, and statistical quality

---

1 Computerworld, September 19, 1988, pg. 2.

control (Garvin, 1987). A significant amount of work on quality management for corporate productivity has been conducted in the field of manufacturing (Fine & Bridge, 1987).

Few corporations, however, have learned how to manage their data quality systematically. We have surveyed a wide spectrum of literature (Carlyle, 1990; Johnson, 1990; Kaplan, 1990; Laudon, 1986; Oman & Ayers, 1988) and found that the issue of data quality has not been addressed methodologically to date.

1.2 A Methodology for Understanding Data Quality

In order to address issues involved in data quality, we have employed a combination of case studies (Bonoma, 1985; Churchill, 1990; Lee, 1989), questionnaires, and analogies from the manufacturing field. Over thirty-five organizations were interviewed, including in-depth studies of four organizations which we will call Integrated Manufacturing, Bullish Securities, Mayflower Bank, and Puritan Hospital in this paper. An iterative approach, consisting of the following stages, was taken: (1) preliminary field studies, (2) identification of data quality parameters, (3) formulation of critical success factors for managing data quality, (4) second round of field studies which included a data quality survey, (5) analysis of field study results, and (6) formulation of recommendations for data quality management.

1.3 The Relationship to Manufacturing Quality

It is interesting to note that there exists a fundamental analogy between quality management in a manufacturing systems environment and an information systems environment. Figure 1 illustrates the analogy between manufacturing systems and information systems. This analogy provides a rich source of parallels to principles of quality management established in the manufacturing literature. Throughout this paper, whenever relevant, we will draw upon this body of knowledge to develop a research foundation for data quality.

	Manufacturing	Information Technology
Input	Material	Data
Process	Line	Software

Figure 1 The analogy between manufacturing and information systems

1.4 Paper Organization

Section 2 summarizes results from our field studies regarding the impact of data quality on corporate profitability. Section 3 identifies the dimensions of data quality. Section 4 presents the survey results in detail and describes the significance of these results. Section 5 presents a framework for organizational change within which IS departments can implement the principles of data quality management. Section 6 presents a set of critical success factors (CSFs) for operationalizing data quality management. Concluding remarks are made in Section 7.

2. The Impact of Data Quality on Corporate Profits

We have focused on three primary areas where data quality impacts corporate profits: customer service, management support, and productivity, as presented below.

2.1 Customer Service

When poor data quality results in poor customer service, there can be a direct negative impact on the bottom line. For example, Integrated Manufacturing is one of the largest providers of optical fiber in the world. Because of the enormous variety of fiber produced, an automated computer system is used to mark fiber before shipment to customers. In early 1990, a *data accuracy* problem caused the system to mislabel a fiber shipment which subsequently was installed under a lake in the state of Washington. When the fiber malfunctioned, the company was forced to pay $500,000 for the removal of the cable, replacement of the experimental fibers, rebundling of the cable, and reinstallation of the cable. Although Integrated Manufacturing did everything it could to correct the problem, the damage to the company's reputation for customer service and quality is a serious problem.

2.2 Management Support

Because it is strategic to an organization's success, the management decision making arena offers the most potential for data quality to impact the bottom line. With the proliferation of Management Support Systems (Rockart & Short, 1989), more and more of the information which top management relies on to guide its thinking will originate from databases both within and across organizational boundaries. As a result, maintaining the quality of the data which drives these systems will become a critical issue.

Bullish Securities, a major New York investment bank, illustrates the tremendous financial value of data in such Management Support Systems. Recently, the bank implemented a risk management system to gather information documenting all of the securities positions at the firm. With *accurate and timely* data, the system serves as a tool which executives use to monitor the firm's exposure to various market risks. However, when critical data is mis-managed, the system can fail to prevent major disasters. For example, during a recent incident, *data availability and timeliness* problems caused the risk management system to fail to alert management of an extremely large exposure to an interest rate sensitive security. As a result, when interest rates changed dramatically, Bullish was caught unaware and absorbed a net loss totalling more than $250 million.

2.3 Productivity

As shown earlier in Figure 1, a manufacturing system can be viewed as a process acting on input material to produce output material. Analogously, an information system can be viewed as a process acting on input data to produce output data. For the information systems (IS) professional, the direct link between quality and productivity in the manufacturing world implies similar consequences for the data center. It is estimated that 40% of IS costs result from quality related problems[2]. For many large organizations, this adds up to hundreds of millions of dollars each year wasted on unproductive reruns, downtime, redundant data entry, and inspection. Effective data quality management offers the potential to dramatically reduce those costs.

---

2 Source: Merrill Lynch, October 1990.

3. The Dimensions of Data Quality

For a manufacturing firm, the concept of quality encompasses much more than material defects. Garvin, a leading authority in manufacturing quality, has developed an analytic framework encompassing eight dimensions of quality: performance, features, reliability, conformance, durability, serviceability, aesthetics, and perceived quality (Garvin, 1988). Likewise, data quality encompasses much more than simply the accuracy of the data stored in corporate files and databases.

3.1 Data Quality Parameters

Based on the attributes revealed in our field research, we have identified four parameters of data quality: accuracy, interpretability, availability, and timeliness. Examples of data quality problems along each of these four parameters appears below.

Data Quality Parameters

Accuracy	Interpretability	Availability	Timeliness
30% of the addresses in an insurance company's customer database are incorrect.	A manufacturer cannot accurately measure its margins because each division defines them differently.	A bank cannot evaluate its real estate exposure because vital information is stored in incompatible data definitions.	Hospital capacity under-utilized because of delays updating admissions information about bed availability.

3.1.1 Accuracy

Accuracy measures the correctness of the information stored in data, a concept which has been referred to as data integrity by the database community (Codd, 1970; Codd, 1979; Codd, 1982; Codd, 1986). In addition to correctness, it includes such data quality problems as inconsistency and redundancy. In the manufacturing world, poor accuracy is analogous to material which does not meet specification. In this manner, accuracy is most closely related to Garvin's dimension of conformance.

Example. Bullish Securities executes upwards of 20,000 stock trades per day for its customers. Most of these orders come in over the phone and must be entered into the systems. Although the data entry process is 99% accurate, in this case that margin of error still leaves the firm exposed to substantial risk. Trades which are executed incorrectly are put into an error account which is owned by the bank. The average value of a trade (across both institutional and retail) is at least $50,000. At a 1% error rate, roughly 200 trades per day are executed incorrectly resulting in $10,000,000 of the firm's capital tied up in the error account Given the volatile nature of the stock market today, this is not an acceptable risk.

3.1.2 Interpretability

Interpretability measures how easy it is to extract understandable information from the data Many factors such as data definitions, report formats, and information processing algorithms impact the interpretability of data As anyone who has ever tried to sift through a one hundred page stack of computer printout knows, data can be accurate, but remain totally un-interpretable and therefore useless In the manufacturing world, poor interpretability is analogous to a product that meets functional specifications but which is too difficult or complicated to use In the Garvin framework, interpretability is most closely related to the concept of performance

Example. Recently, the CEO of Integrated Manufacturing set a 10% operating margins goal for each of the four divisions. Although all divisions met the goal, the company as a whole did not realize a 10% operating margin. After some investigation, it was determined that the corporate headquarters and each division had different definitions of operating margins. In this case, the lack of consensus regarding data definitions hindered the interpretability of data: the data provided to corporate by the operating divisions was very difficult to interpret with respect to the corporate definition of operating margin

3.1.3 Availability

Availability measures how quickly information stored in corporate data can be gathered by the people who need it One very important aspect of availability addresses the ease with which information stored in systems and databases within and across organizational boundaries can be brought together for analysis and reference. This is often referred to as the data integration problem. In the manufacturing world, availability is analogous to a product's susceptibility to "downtime" the amount of time a product is unavailable for use because of scheduled or unscheduled maintenance In this manner, availability is closest to Garvin's concepts of serviceability and durability.

Example. Like many commercial banks, The Mayflower Bank is concerned about the financial health of their real estate portfolio. This is particularly true at a time when federal regulators are taking a closer look at real estate lending across the country In order for IS to build a real estate portfolio system which could monitor the financial status of the bank's loans, data needed to be accessed from the commercial loan system (when lending information resides) and the real estate appraisal system (where current asset valuations reside) Unfortunately, these two systems use incompatible data definitions and, as a result, it remains very difficult to build the necessary real estate portfolio system

3.1.4 Timeliness

Timeliness measures how up to date the information stored in the database is In many situations, this can be more important than accuracy For example, a 99% accurate, but up to date, mailing list is much more valuable than a 100% accurate, but five year old, mailing list. Within manufacturing, timeliness issues have the largest impact on materials management For example, in the age of just-in-time manufacturing, a supplier's quality rating is based largely on how adept he is at meeting delivery schedules By analogy to Garvin's framework, timeliness comprises another facet of performance.

Example. Within hospitals, the timeliness of information reporting patient conditions and availability of beds is critical for effective and efficient administration of health care. Toward this end, Puritan Hospital, a leading New England hospital, is developing a Bed Control System which will provide an accurate, up-to-the-minute census of available beds within each floor and unit This will greatly improve the staff's coordination of "patient flow" (admissions, discharges, transfers), allow doctors and nurses to easily locate patients, and allow housekeeping and other services to schedule work more efficiently. Currently, the hospital takes census every midnight and manually manages the daily use of beds.

3.2 The Data Value Chain

During the course of the investigations, it became apparent that different organizations had widely different needs with respect to data quality management In general, these needs varied with the economic function being performed in the *data value chain*, as shown in Figure 2 In this manner, the data value chain represents a division of organizations into three groups with respect to their data function.

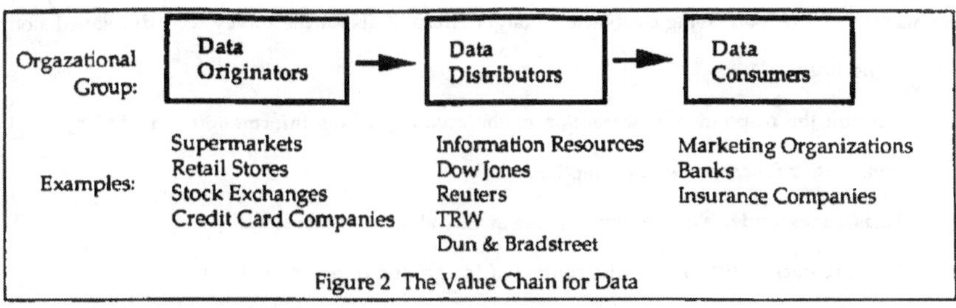

Figure 2 The Value Chain for Data

Data originators are those organizations which generate data having value to other organizations. Supermarkets which collect and resell point-of-sale data constitute one example. Data distributors purchase data from the originators and resell it to consuming organizations. Information Resources, Inc. (IRI) is an excellent example of a data distributor. They purchase point-of-sale data from supermarkets, analyze and process it, and then resell it to consumer marketing firms such as General Mills. Finally, consuming organizations are those which acquire data generated externally. Banks offer an example of data consumers because they buy credit data from distributors such as TRW and Dun & Bradstreet.

With the exception of distributors, most companies do not belong solely to one group or another. In fact, most large corporations are very vertically integrated with respect to data. Frequently, different departments within an organization will perform different functions with respect to data. For example, marketing organizations consume data on customer buying habits from information compiled by the finance organization. In addition, this information is frequently supplemented with data purchased from a distributor. As a result of vertical integration, most IS organizations have responsibility for data origination, internal distribution, and consumption. More and more, they also have responsibility for purchasing and integrating data from distributors.

3.3 Targeting Organizations Vertically Integrated with Respect to Data

Because this research focuses on data quality management from an IS perspective, our survey targeted organizations which are vertically integrated with respect to data. In this manner, the target audience for the survey was corporate level IS staff, preferably high level executives or Data Base Administrators (DBA's). Having established a target group, goals for the survey were developed along the following lines:

- Capture the respondent's perception of the accuracy of the information provided by the IS organization for corporate consumption.
- Measure respondents' perceptions of data quality along its dimensions.
- Measure data availability in the context of integrating departmental data.
- Understand the level of difficulty involved in tracking down data quality problems.

4. Data Quality Survey Results

In what follows, we present the key survey results with respect to each of these goals. The histogram below indicates the distribution of the 24 survey respondents across industries.

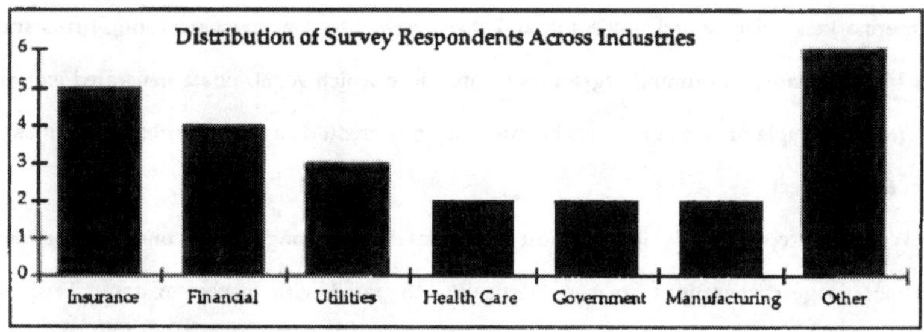

4.1 Detailed Survey Results

Since each survey goal corresponds to a particular survey question, the following sections each begin with that survey question presented in italics.

4.1.1 Frequency of Errors in IS Products and Services

Consider the information products and services such as reports, decision support systems, accounting records, customer files, customer service, mailing lists, which are produced from corporate data. How accurate are these products?

- ☐.....*100%* *Information products and services never contain errors.*
- ☐.....*99%* *Information products and services rarely contain errors.*
- ☐.....*95%* *Information products and services occasionally contain errors.*
- ☐.....*90%* *Information products and services frequently contain errors.*
- ☐....*below 90%* *Information products and services are always with errors.*

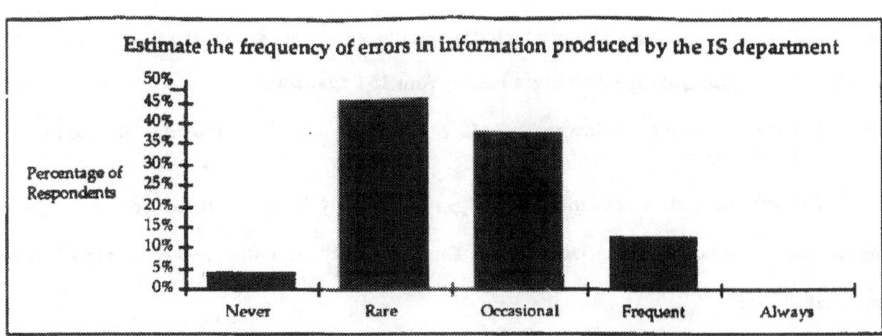

Responses to this question indicate that over half of the participating organizations rate their products and services at 95% accuracy or less.

4.1.2 Ratings of Accuracy, Interpretability, Availability, and Timeliness

Consider the data underlying these information products and services. Accuracy measures the correctness of the information stored in data. Interpretability measures how easy it is to extract understandable information from the data. Availability measures how quickly information stored in corporate data can be gathered by the people who need it. Timeliness measures how up to date the information stored in the data is. Please estimate the quality of your corporate data along these four parameters.

Accuracy: ☐ *Excellent.* ☐ *Good.* ☐ *Fair.* ☐ *Poor.* ☐ *Terrible.*
Interpretability: ☐ *Excellent.* ☐ *Good.* ☐ *Fair.* ☐ *Poor.* ☐ *Terrible.*
Availability: ☐ *Excellent.* ☐ *Good.* ☐ *Fair.* ☐ *Poor.* ☐ *Terrible.*
Timeliness: ☐ *Excellent.* ☐ *Good.* ☐ *Fair.* ☐ *Poor.* ☐ *Terrible.*

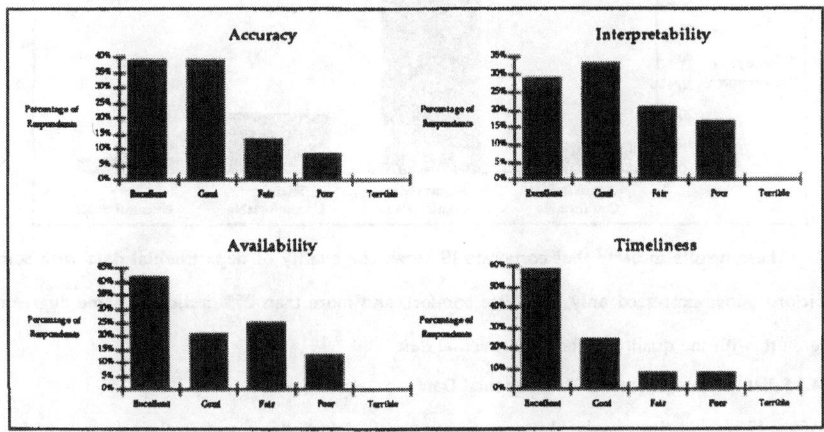

These responses indicate that IS organizations currently view interpretability and availability as the parameters along which data quality problems are most acute.

4.1.3 Major Data Quality Challenges Facing Your IS Organization

List the three major challenges your IS organization faces in maintaining the quality of corporate data.

This question does not lend itself to graphical analysis, so the responses of the participating organizations have been summarized below. The four most frequently cited challenges to maintaining data quality are:

- Assigning responsibility for data quality.
- Managing data in a decentralized environment.
- Insuring the quality of data feeds (e.g., data entry or third party data).
- Converting data into usable information.

4.1.4 Comfort with Quality of Departmental Data

Consider the data stored and maintained within your company's various departments. How comfortable do you feel about using this data?

☐.....*Absolutely comfortable. Important business decisions are based on this data.*
☐.....*Moderately comfortable. Suitable for informal analysis and internal use.*
☐.....*Slightly uncomfortable. Check twice before using it for anything important.*
☐.....*Very Uncomfortable. The departmental data is almost unusable.*

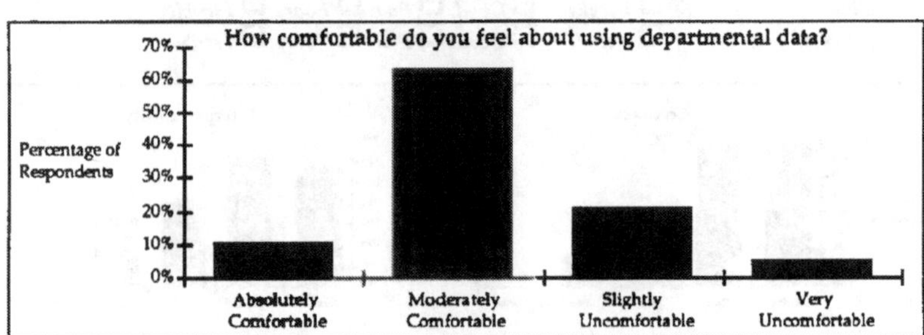

These results indicate that corporate IS views the quality of departmental data with some suspicion. Most expressed only moderate comfort, and more than 25% indicated some degree of discomfort, with the quality of the departmental data.

4.1.5 Ease of Integration for Departmental Data

Many IS organizations would like to be able to use the information stored in their departmental databases for corporate or inter-departmental purposes. (e.g., building inter-departmental applications or decision support systems) How easy is it for your IS organization to use data stored in departmental databases?

☐ *Very easy* ☐ *Easy* ☐ *Somewhat difficult* ☐ *Difficult* ☐ *Impossible*

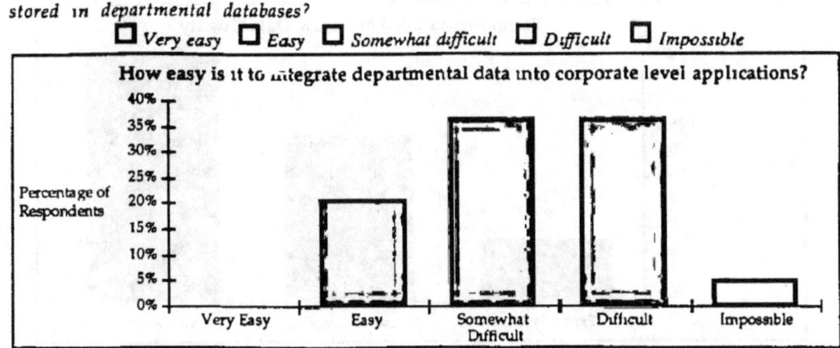

The responses to this question clearly indicate significant availability problems with respect to departmental data. In fact, most IS organizations are implementing technologies and procedures designed to improve departmental data integration

4.1.6 Data Auditability

When data quality problems are discovered, how easy is it to track down the source?

☐ *Very easy* ☐ *Easy* ☐ *Somewhat difficult* ☐ *Difficult* ☐ *Impossible*

How easy is it to track down data quality problems?

30%
25%
20%
15%
10%
5%
0%
Percentage of Respondents
Very Easy
Easy
Somewhat Difficult
Difficult
Impossible

Responses to this question reveal that tracking down the sources of data quality can be difficult This result points to an emerging need for some technology to address the issue of data auditability

4.1 7 Use of Technology

Which of the following technologies does your company use to ensure data quality?

☐ *Expert Systems* ☐ *Statistical Sampling* ☐ *Human verification*

☐ *Other* ______________________________

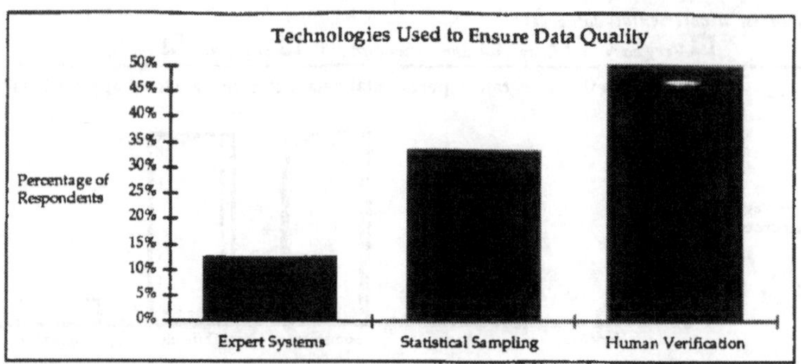

Responses to this question show that automation of the data quality inspection process is still in its infancy. The reliance on human inspection as a means of controlling defects is the hallmark of an immature quality management effort (Crosby, 1979).

4.2 Observations and Caveats Relating to Survey Results

When interpreting any set of data, the biases of the source must be taken into consideration. In many cases, truthful answers to the questions could reflect very poorly on the respondents. Since our survey was aimed at IS managers responsible for the systems and data under discussion, the data may represent a more optimistic vision of America's corporate data quality problem than an unbiased source might offer. Bearing this in mind, we summarize our research results below:

- Over 50% of the respondents rated the accuracy of the information produced by the IS department at 95% or less. When the people who manage the data are willing to admit significant problems exist, it indicates that data quality is probably quite bad. This observation is further supported by our experience during interviews where many IS professionals admitted privately that data quality problems are pervasive.
- Interpretability and availability were judged to be the parameters along which data quality problems are most significant.
- Inconsistent data standards across departments are broadly admitted to be a major problem facing IS organizations.
- On the issue of departmental data, where our survey respondents may have felt freer to be

honest, there was considerable criticism. Almost 90% of the respondents maintained that departmental data was not of suitable quality to base important business decisions. Over 25% recommended not using departmental data for *anything* important unless it was checked twice.

- Assigning responsibility for data quality within the organization is a top priority of most IS departments.
- A majority of respondents expressed difficulty in tracking down the sources of their data quality problems.

5. Managing Data Quality

We have presented an analogy between quality management in manufacturing and information systems. In the manufacturing world, significant improvements in productivity and customer service have resulted in 4 - 8 fold reductions in the total cost of quality (Crosby, 1979; Garvin, 1988). Since most IS organizations have little or no formal systems for data quality management, we postulate that the opportunities for improvement and resulting economic gain in the area of data quality management are tremendous. Such improvement, however, cannot be achieved without significant organizational changes. Following Tribus (Tribus, 1989), an authority on the implementation of Deming's quality management principles (Deming, 1986), we group the required organizational changes into five categories below based on our field studies:

(1). Clearly articulate a data quality vision in business terms.

(2). Establish central responsibility for data quality within IS.

(3). Educate project and systems managers.

(4). Teach new data quality skills to the entire IS organization.

(5). Institutionalize continuous data quality improvement.

5.1 Clearly Articulate a Data Quality Vision in Business Terms

In order to improve quality, one must first set standards. At the highest levels, standards are set by users: the external and internal customers for the data produced by information systems. Such standards are expressed in business terms. In this manner, the first step toward implementing a data quality improvement plan is for top IS management to clearly articulate a data quality vision in business terms. The following example from Mayflower Bank's 1990 Data Administration Task Force report illustrates this principle very well: *"Customer service and decision making at Mayflower Bank will be unconstrained by the availability, accessibility, or accuracy of data held in automated form on any strategic platform."*

Since leadership is crucial in the early stages of any quality improvement program, the data quality vision must be clearly identified with the top level management within information systems. At this stage, top management's goal is to begin organizational awareness of data quality problems and start everybody moving in the same direction. Toward this end, the chief information officer (CIO) must make it clear to the entire organization that data quality has become a top priority.

5.2 Establish Central Responsibility for Data Quality Within IS

Once a vision has been articulated, the organization needs to establish central responsibility for data quality. Ultimately, this responsibility rests with the CIO, but another person, reporting directly to the CIO, needs to be given day to day responsibility for data quality. Many organizations are tempted to proclaim that data quality is "everybody's responsibility", but in practice this approach leads to confusion and inaction. Implementing a data quality improvement program requires significant organizational change as well as the adoption of new management techniques and technologies. For these reasons, a data administrator[3] must be given responsibility and authority for ensuring data quality explicitly.

Data administration should be a managerial, rather than technical, function distinct from data base administration. The data administrator is responsible for making sure that data resources are managed to meet business needs. In this manner, data quality falls naturally within this sphere of responsibility. The data administrator should head up the data administration staff which serves as a center of expertise on the application of quality management within the IS organization. In most organizations today, data administration remains a fairly low level function concerned primarily with the development of data models. In the future, organizations will need to enhance the power and

3 Date, C.J., *An Introduction to Database Systems*, Addison-Wesley, 1990, pg. 14.

prestige of the data administration position in order to provide a credible and effective center of responsibility for data quality management.

Figure 3 indicates that the data administrator has responsibilities spread equally across the two highest levels of quality management breakthroughs and iterative improvements (Juran & Gryna, 1980) In the area of breakthroughs, the data administrator coordinates work with the CIO and senior level management to identify systems redesign projects and new technologies which could have tremendous impact on the organization's management of data quality In terms of iterative improvements, the data administrator serves as a central source of information and guidance which project and systems managers can access regarding data quality matters

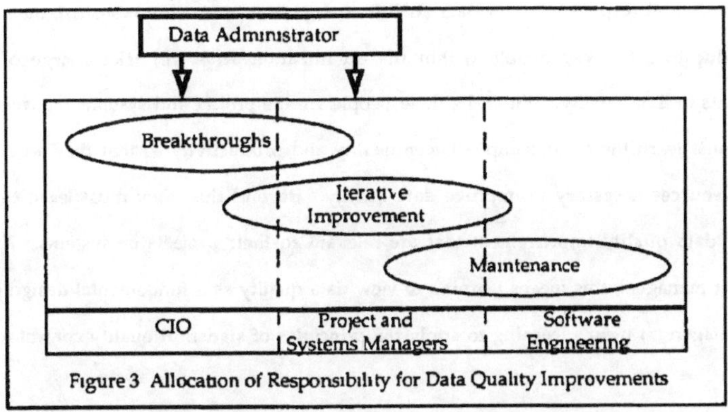

Figure 3 Allocation of Responsibility for Data Quality Improvements

Our case studies illustrate the variety of approaches organizations are taking to assigning responsibility for data quality For example, Mayflower Bank has outlined a breakthrough technological initiative centered around the creation of a data administrator position The data administrator will be responsible for the development and installation of a *data delivery utility architecture* for corporate data. As the corporation's official source of data, this system's primary function will be to serve as a regulated, central repository for data storage and standards enforcement Updating and accessing the information stored there will occur via a set of technologies designed to insure data quality.

On the other hand, Integrated Manufacturing has failed to perceive the importance of centralizing authority and is instead attempting to push responsibility for accurate data back to the source. This is in line with their corporate quality goals to ensure quality at the source and not build inspection into a product or process. While minimizing reliance on inspection is an important goal, Integrated seems to be forgetting Deming's fundamental lesson that management should hold primary responsibility for ensuring quality (Deming, 1986). Manufacturing research has shown conclusively that most quality problems result from poor systems design and administration and are therefore the responsibility of management.

5.3 Educate Project and Systems Managers

Once central responsibility for data quality management has been established, the stage is set to begin educating the key people within the organization who will take charge of iterative improvements in data quality. Within IS, these people are the project and systems managers. These managers must learn the relationship between quality and productivity so that they will invest the time and resources necessary to improve data quality. Beyond this, they must learn the specific methods of data quality improvement that are relevant to their projects or systems. For project development managers, this means learning to view data quality as a fundamental design goal. For systems managers, it means learning to apply the principles of statistical quality control to monitor systems.

5.4 Teach New Data Quality Skills to the Entire IS Organization

Responsibility for the successful implementation and maintenance of data quality programs belongs to the entire organization. Hence, the entire IS organization must learn the skills required to put data quality improvement programs into place. The skills required by an individual will vary according to his or her responsibilities.

In general, data quality responsibilities will fall into one or more of the following three categories: inspection and data entry, process control, and systems design. Knowledge of statistical quality control (SQC) is essential for work in all three areas and therefore SQC techniques must be universally understood throughout the IS organization. Below we discuss the three categories of data quality responsibility and the relevant skills required for each.

Inspection and Data Entry. Inspection and data entry involves responsibility for the accuracy of data as it is entered into a system or is processed by a system. Current practice for the inspection of data remains mostly manual. Modern interactive and forms-based user interfaces require training in order to fulfill their potential for minimizing data entry accuracy problems. For example, Mayflower Bank has established corporate policies urging that:

- Data should be entered into machine form only once, and this should be accomplished as close as possible to the point of origin of that data.
- Newly entered data should be subjected to automated edits, consistency checks, and audits as appropriate.

Process Control. Process control involves maintaining and monitoring the performance of existing systems with respect to data quality management. In addition to SQC, the training required here involves the use of auditability tools for tracking down the source of data quality problems. In our survey, over 50% of respondents expressed difficulty in tracking down the sources of data quality problems. In addition, case studies indicate that people with process control responsibilities frequently need training in the proper procedures for the uploading and downloading of data. In this regard, Mayflower has determined that any uploading of data to the mainframe requires the same editing and consistency checks required of newly entered data.

Systems Design. Finally, systems design involves building new systems or upgrading existing applications with data quality management as a primary design goal. In this area there are a host of tools and techniques which professional IS developers should learn in order to design systems which are compatible with data quality goals (e.g., CASE tools, data modeling, intelligent user interface design, data warehouses, and auditability tools).

With respect to systems design, many organizations are moving toward the conception of a *data warehouse* (Devlin & Murphy, 1988) as a means of ensuring data quality for future applications. For example, Integrated Manufacturing is in the process of developing and installing a data warehouse. Achieving this will require corporate IS to define which data is needed from the divisions, how often to upload it, and where it should reside. In this manner, the data warehouse addresses interpretability, availability, and timeliness as well as accuracy.

5.5 Institutionalize Continuous Data Quality Improvement

Once the entire organization has received the necessary training, and data quality improvement plans have been put into action, it is necessary for top management to ensure that the data quality improvement process becomes institutionalized. This requires leadership from the CIO and other top management in the form of visible continuous interest in data quality activities. For example, regular meetings, presentations, and reporting structures should be established to track the organization's progress in meeting data quality goals. Additionally, data quality improvement projects need to become a regular part of the budgetary process.

6. Operationalizing Data Quality Management

In order to define continuous improvement projects, organizations should focus on *critical success factors* (Bullen & Rockart, 1981) in order to identify operational objectives which are critical for the successful management of data quality. Based on interviews and surveys, five critical success factors have been identified: (1) Certify Existing Corporate Data, (2) Standardize Data Definitions, (3) Certify External Sources of Data, (4) Control Internal Generation of Data, and (5) Provide Data Auditability.

Figure 4 illustrates which systems and data sources the five critical success factors impact. In this example, the goal of the IS organization is to ensure that the corporate level data exhibits superior quality across all four parameters: accuracy, availability, interpretability, and timeliness.

Certifying the existing data implies providing a guarantee that the corporate data, depicted in the center, is 100% accurate. Standardizing data definitions ensures that all data flows, indicated by the arrows, among internal data sources can be implemented in a straightforward manner. The result is a high degree of availability for corporate data. Certifying external sources of data involves ensuring that none of the sources depicted in the outer ring are contributing accuracy errors to the corporate data. Likewise, controlling internal data generation implies certifying all of the applications depicted in the inner circle, and their interfaces with the corporate data. Finally, providing data auditability implies that when data quality problems are detected in the corporate data, they can be traced to the source, whether it be internal or external.

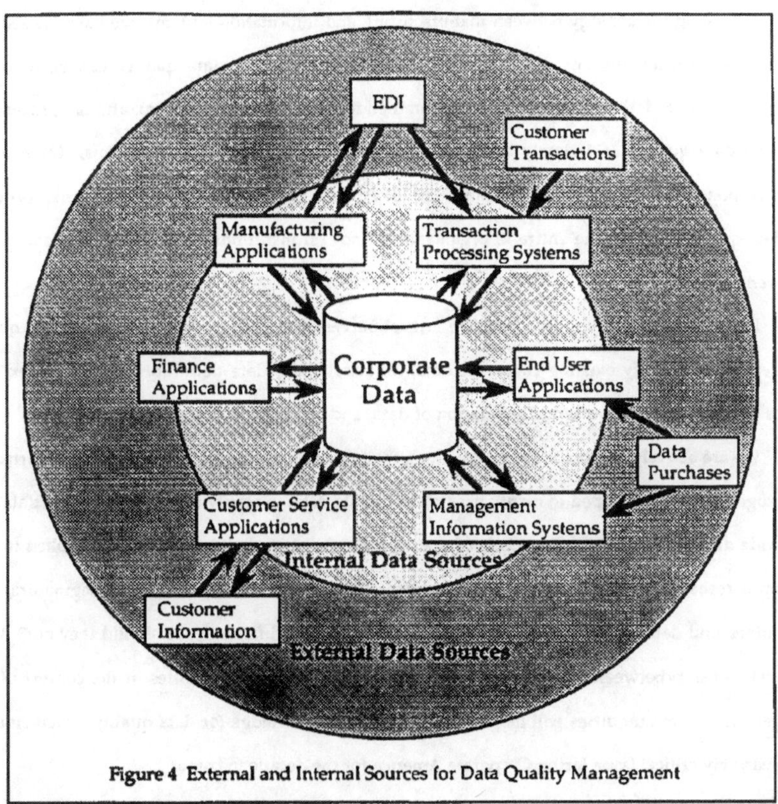

Figure 4 External and Internal Sources for Data Quality Management

7. Summary and Future Directions

In this paper, we have introduced a fundamental analogy between manufacturing and information systems, defined the dimensions of data quality, and developed the concept of a *data value chain*. Based on these ideas, we have described the impact of data quality on corporate profits and presented a detailed field study on data quality. Our study revealed that Corporate America's data quality can be improved in terms of interpretability, availability, and timeliness as well as accuracy We have also identified tracking down the sources of data quality problems as a major impediment to successful data quality management.

Following the analogy between manufacturing and information systems, we have argued that there is a significant amount of economic benefit to be gained if data quality can be managed effectively Toward that end, we have recommended the following organizational process for managing data quality: (1) clearly articulate a data quality vision in business terms, (2) establish central responsibility for data quality within IS, (3) educate project and systems managers, (4) teach new data quality skills to the entire IS organization, and (5) institutionalize continuous data quality improvement

In addition, we have identified five critical success factors for operationalizing data quality management (1) certify existing corporate data, (2) standardize data definitions, (3) certify external sources of data, (4) control internal generation of data, and (5) provide data auditability.

We are actively conducting research along the following directions· What kinds of information technologies can be developed to certify existing corporate data; to certify external sources of data; and to provide data auditability? What kinds of operations management techniques can be applied to help develop a research foundation for data quality management? How should data originators, data distributors, and data consumers manage data quality problems differently, or should they not? What is the relationship between data quality and the corresponding data attributes in the context of risk management? These inquiries will help develop a body of knowledge for data quality management -- an increasingly critical issue facing Corporate America for the decade to come.

8. References

[1] Bonoma, T. V. (1985) Case research in marketing opportunities, problems, and a process *Journal of Marketing Research, 22*, pp 199-208

[2] Bullen, C. & Rockart, J (1981) *A Primer on Critical Successful Factors* (WP#69) Center for Information Systems Research, MIT June 1981

[3] Carlyle, R (1990) Is Your Data Ready For the Repository? *Datamation*, , pp 43-47.

[4] Cash, J I & Konsynski, B R (1985) IS redraws competitive boundaries *Harvard Business Review*, 63(2), pp 134-142

[5] Churchill, G (1990) *Market Research Methodologies* (5th ed.). Dryden Press.

[6] Clemens, E (1988) McKesson drug company a case study of economost, a strategic information system. *Journal of Management Information Systems*, 5(1), pp 141-149

[7] Codd, E F (1970). A relational model of data for large shared data banks. *Communications of the ACM*, 13(6), pp. 377-387

[8] Codd, E F (1979) Extending the relational database model to capture more meaning *ACM Transactions on Database Systems*, 4(4), pp 397-434

[9] Codd, E. F. (1982). Relational database. A practical foundation for productivity, the 1981 ACM Turing Award Lecture *Communications of the ACM*, 25(2), pp. 109-117.

[10] Codd, E. F (1986) *An evaluation scheme for database management systems that are claimed to be relational*. Los Angeles, CA. 1986. pp 720-729.

[11] Crosby, P B (1979) *Quality is Free* New York McGraw-Hill

[12] Deming, E W (1986) *Out of the Crisis* . Center for Advanced Engineering Study, MIT.

[13] Devlin, B. A. & Murphy, P T (1988). An architecture for a business and information system *IBM Systems Journal*, 27(1), pp. 60-80

[14] Fine, C H & Bridge, D H (1987) *Quest for Quality* (1 ed) Industrial Engineering and Management Press

[15] Garvin, D. A. (1983). Quality on the line. *Harvard Business Review*, (September- October), pp 65-75

[16] Garvin, D. A. (1987). Competing on the eight dimensions of quality. *Harvard Business Review*, (November-December), pp 101-109

[17] Garvin, D. A. (1988). *Managing Quality-The Strategic and Competitive Edge* (1 ed) New York· The Free Press.

[18] Goodhue, D. L., Quillard, J A., & Rockart, J F (1988) Managing The Data Resources A Contingency Perspective. *MIS Quarterly*, 12(3), pp 373-392

[19] Henderson, J. C. (1989) *Building and sustaining partnership between line and I/S managers* (CISR WP #195) 1989.

[20] Ives, B. & Learmonth, G P. (1984) The information system as a competitive weapon *Communications of the ACM*, 27, pp. 1193-1201

[21] Johnson, J R (1990). Hallmark's Formula For Quality *Datamation*, , pp. 119-122.

[22] Juran, J. M & Gryna, F M. (1980). *Quality Planning and Analysis* (2nd ed.). New York McGraw Hill.

[23] Kaplan, R S. (1990) The Four-Stage Model of Cost Systems Design *Management Accounting, 71*(8), pp. 22-26.

[24] Keen, P. G. W. (1986) *Competing In Time Using Telecommunications For Competitive Advantage* (1 ed) Ballinger

[25] Laudon, K. C (1986) Data Quality and Due Process in Large Interorganizational Record Systems *Communications of the ACM*, 29(1), pp 4-11

[26] Lee, A. (1989) A Scientific Methodology for MIS Case Studies *Management Information Systems Quarterly, 13*(1), pp. 33-50

[27] Madnick, S , Osborn, C , & Wang, Y R (1990) Motivating Strategic Alliances for Composite Information Systems the case of a major regional hospital *Journal of Management Information Systems, 6*(4), pp 99-117

[28] Madnick, S E. & Wang, Y R (1988) Evolution towards strategic applications of databases through composite information systems. *Journal of Management Information Systems, 5*(2), pp. 5-22

[29] McFarlan, F. W (1984) Information technology changes the way you compete. *Harvard Business Review, 62*(2), pp 98-105.

[30] Oman, R C & Ayers, T B (1988) Improving Data Quality *Journal of Systems Management, 39*(5), pp 31-35

[31] Rockart, J. F & Short, J E. (1989) IT in the 1990s Managing Organizational Interdependence *Sloan Management Review, Sloan School of Management, MIT, 30*(2), pp 7-17

[32] Scott Morton, M. (1989). *Management in the 1990s Research Program Final Report*. 1989.

[33] Tribus, M (1989) *Quality First* . National Society of Professional Engineers

www.ingramcontent.com/pod-product-compliance
Lightning Source LLC
LaVergne TN
LVHW052018160826
845678LV00003B/1096

* 9 7 8 0 3 5 3 2 7 4 1 6 7 *